Capital Punishment

Critical World Issues

Abortion
Animal Rights
The Arms Trade
Capital Punishment
Consumerism
Drugs
Equal Opportunities
Euthanasia

Food Technology
Genetic Engineering
Genocide
Human Rights
Poverty
Racism
Refugees
Terrorism

CRITICAL WORLD ISSUES

Capital Punishment

Adam Ward

MASON CREST
PHILADELPHIA

30842 3175
C

Mason Crest
450 Parkway Drive, Suite D
Broomall, PA 19008
www.masoncrest.com

Printed and bound in the United States of America.

CPSIA Compliance Information: Batch #CWI2016.
For further information, contact Mason Crest at 1-866-MCP-Book.

First printing
1 3 5 7 9 8 6 4 2

Library of Congress Cataloging-in-Publication Data

on file at the Library of Congress
ISBN: 978-1-4222-3649-9 (hc)
ISBN: 978-1-4222-8129-1 (ebook)

Critical World Issues series ISBN: 978-1-4222-3645-1

Table of Contents

KEY ICONS TO LOOK FOR:

Words to Understand: These words with their easy-to-understand definitions will increase the reader's understanding of the text, while building vocabulary skills.

Sidebars: This boxed material within the main text allows readers to build knowledge, gain insights, explore possibilities, and broaden their perspectives by weaving together additional information to provide realistic and holistic perspectives.

Research Projects: Readers are pointed toward areas of further inquiry connected to each chapter. Suggestions are provided for projects that encourage deeper research and analysis.

Text-Dependent Questions: These questions send the reader back to the text for more careful attention to the evidence presented there.

Series Glossary of Key Terms: This back-of-the book glossary contains terminology used throughout this series. Words found here increase the reader's ability to read and comprehend higher-level books and articles in this field.

THE STATE OF TEXAS
VS.

Kenneth W. Stokes aka Gary Graham

315 E. Rosamond #12
Houston, Texas

FELONY CHARGE:

Agg Robbery FIVE COUNTS

CAUSE NO.: 335136

HARRIS COUNTY DISTRICT COURT NO.: 177th

REV. 5/8

SPN: _____
DOB: W/M 9-5-60
or 1-22-61

DATE PREPARED: 5-22-81 BY: sd DA NO. 06
AGENCY: HPD O/R NO.: 25649281
NCIC CODE: 1201-04-09 ARREST DATE: 5-20-81
RELATED CASES:

2 BAIL $ 20,000.00 each count
PRIOR CAUSE NO.: _____

WAIVER OF CONSTITUTIONAL RIGHTS, AGREEMENT TO STIPULATE, AND JUDICIAL CONFESSION

In open court and prior to entering my plea, I waive the right of trial by jury. I also waive the appearance, confrontation, and cross-examination of witnesses, and my right against self-incrimination. The charges against me allege that in Harris County, Texas, I

KENNETH W. STOKES AKA GARY GRAHAM

May 16, 1931

hereafter styled the Defendant, heretofore on or about _____, d

then and there unlawfully

while in the course of committing theft of property owned by Joseph Carl Raposa, hereafter styled the Complainant, and with intent to obtain and maintain control of the property, intentionally and knowingly threaten and place the Complainant in fear of imminent bodily injury and death, by using and exhibiting a deadly weapon, namely, a firearm.

COUNT II

It is further presented that in Harris County, Texas, Kenneth W. Stokes aka Gary Graham, hereafter styled the Defendant heretofore on or about, May 18, 1981, did then and there unlawfully while in the course of committing theft of property owned by Ernest Doakes, hereafter styled the Complainant, and with intent to obtain and maintain control of the property, intentionally and knowingly threaten and place the Complainant in fear of imminent bodily injury and death, by using and exhibiting a deadly weapon, namely, a firearm.

COUNT III

It is further presented that in Harris County, Texas, Kenneth W. Stokes aka Gary Graham, hereafter styled the Defendant heretofore on or about, May 18, 1981, did then and there unlawfully while in the course of committing theft of property owned by Charles Powell, hereafter styled the Complainant, and with intent to obtain and maintain control of the property, intentionally and knowingly threaten and place the Complainant in fear of imminent bodily injury and death, by using and exhibiting a deadly weapon, namely, a firearm.

COUNT IV

It is further presented that in Harris County, Texas, Kenneth W. Stokes aka Gary Graham, hereafter styled the Defendant heretofore on or about, May 19, 1981, did then and there unlawfully while in the course of committing theft of property owned by Richard Bowen Sanford, hereafter styled the Complainant, and with intent to obtain and maintain control of the property, intentionally and knowingly threaten and place the Complainant in fear of imminent bodily injury and death, by using and exhibiting a deadly weapon, namely, a firearm.

It is further presented that in Harris County, Texas, Kenneth W. Stokes aka Gary Graham, hereafter styled the Defendant heretofore on or about, May 20, 1981, did then and there unlawfully while in the course of committing theft of property owned by Lisa Blackburn, hereafter styled the Complainant, and with intent to obtain and maintain control of the property, intentionally and knowingly threaten and place the Complainant in fear of imminent bodily injury and death, by using and exhibiting a deadly weapon, namely, a firearm.

AGAINST THE PEACE AND DIGNITY OF THE STATE.

May 16, 1981 - count I
May ___ 1981 - count II

What Is Capital Punishment?

In May 1981, Gary Graham went on a crime spree in Houston, Texas. In a week, he committed nine robberies involving guns and the threat of violence. At his trial, he was accused of murdering Bobby Grant Lambert. Graham pleaded guilty to the robberies but denied murder. Despite flimsy evidence, Graham was convicted of murder and sentenced to death.

From the start, it was clear that Graham had not been well defended at his trial. The main evidence against him was provided by an eyewitness named Bernadine Skillern. However, she was the only one, out of six witnesses, who identified Graham as the killer. Furthermore, the incident took place at night, and Skillern only saw the killer fleetingly. Yet the defense attorney did not *cross-examine* Skillern or challenge her statements. Also, *ballistics* experts could not say with any

Gary Graham's guilty plea to robbery charges stemming from his 1981 crime spree. However, Graham denied being involved in the murder of Bobby Grant Lambert.

certainty whether or not Graham's gun had fired the bullet responsible for the death.

In 1988, four witnesses came forward claiming that Graham had been with them on the night of the murder. An appeal was made against the guilty verdict, but it was turned down. Other holes were then found in the prosecution's case. For example, two of the witnesses claimed the murderer was under 5'3" tall; Graham was 5'10" tall. In all, a total of 33 appeals were made against the verdict, and each one was rejected.

When Graham began his sentence, he was a rebellious young man who frequently fought with his jailers. Over the years, he became more resigned to his fate. He saw himself as a casualty in a war against injustice. When the scheduled date of *execution* drew near, Graham's lawyers made a final appeal for mercy to George W. Bush, who at the time was the state's governor. Bush took the advice of the Texas parole board and turned down the appeal.

 Words to Understand in This Chapter

ballistics—the science that studies the movement of objects (such as bullets or rockets) that are shot or forced to move forward through the air.

capital punishment—the death penalty for a crime.

cross-examine—to question a witness who has already testified in order to check or discredit the witness's testimony, knowledge, or credibility.

execution—the act of killing someone especially as punishment for a crime.

lethal injection—the practice of injecting a combination of poisons into a person with a fatal dose of drugs to cause immediate death.

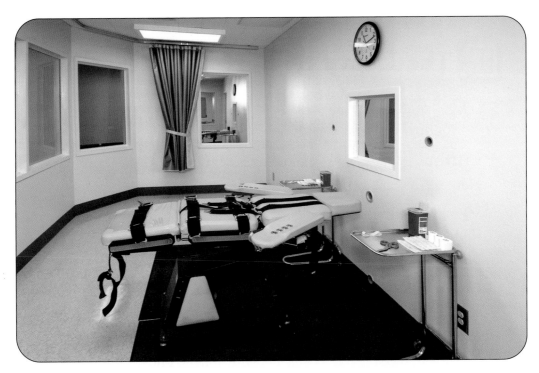

The lethal injection room at San Quentin State Prison in California. The process, in which a combination of drugs are injected into a convicted criminal's veins in order to stop his or her respiration and heart, is the most common form of execution in the United States. Supporters of the practice argue that, unlike previous methods used to execute criminals such as hanging, the electric chair, or the gas chamber, lethal injection is relatively painless, because the criminal is rendered unconscious before the killing drugs are injected. Opponents believe that the drug meant to cause unconsciousness can wear off relatively quickly, meaning that the criminal could be conscious throughout the process.

Graham's execution was to be carried out by *lethal injection*. On the day of the execution, Graham became angry and bitter once again. He had to be subdued by prison guards and carried into the execution room. He was covered in a sheet and restrained as he was injected with the poisonous drugs. He looked over towards one of his supporters, let out a slight groan, then died.

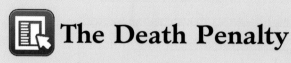

The Death Penalty

Whether ethical or not, the death penalty is legal punishment in countries all over the world.

CHINA sentences more people to death than any other country. Here people are executed for crimes such as murder, robbery, rape, bomb throwing, arson, and sabotage. In 2014, it is believed that at least 3,000 people were executed, though the actual figure may be much higher.

IRAN had the second highest number of executions in 2014, with at least 289 people put to death. The death penalty is popular in this country, and some news articles have claimed that death sentences are imposed because judges are influenced by the opinion of the public.

SAUDI ARABIA accounted for 90 or more executions in 2014, third most in the world. Capital punishment is administered by beheading or stoning for crimes such as murder, terrorism, burglary, and adultery.

The family of Bobby Grant Lambert issued a statement afterwards saying that they were sorry for Graham's family, but they felt that justice had been done.

What Is Capital Punishment?

Capital punishment is the killing of a person as a punishment

With at least 61 instances of capital punishment carried out, **IRAQ** had the fourth highest number in 2014. Criminals are executed by shooting or hanging, although there is not a mandatory death sentence; mitigating circumstances are considered by the courts.

The fifth highest number of executions in 2014 occurred in the **UNITED STATES**, where 35 people were executed. Here the death penalty is imposed only for crimes involving murder. The death penalty is legal in all but 19 states and the District of Columbia; four additional states have a temporary stoppage enacted by the governor.

for committing a crime. The word capital, meaning the top of something, refers to a person's head; in the past, people were often executed by severing their head from their body. Today there are many different kinds of execution, including lethal injection, electrocution, gassing, hanging, shooting, beheading, and stoning.

In many ancient cultures, people who committed serious crimes were executed by stoning. Members of the community would take the transgressor away from their settlement and throw rocks at the person until they were dead.

Capital punishment has been used by societies throughout history. Today the death sentence is most commonly used as a punishment for very serious crimes, such as murder, terrorism, and rape. Whether or not an offense is judged to be a capital crime—a crime that is so terrible that the criminal deserves death—often depends on the culture or religion of a particular state or country.

Capital punishment is an issue that has stirred a great deal of debate in recent times. There are many opponents of the death penalty as well as many others who believe that it is a just form of punishment. In this book, we will look at the arguments for and against capital punishment. We will ask whether it is right for a government to order someone's death and whether this acts as a deterrent to other potential murderers. We will also look at what life is like for those condemned to death.

Is Capital Punishment Fair?

If people agree that capital punishment is just, they must then consider whether it is applied fairly. Does the justice system in a particular country always produce fair verdicts? Do innocent people sometimes get executed? And what about vulnerable groups such as the young, the elderly, pregnant women, foreigners, people with intellectual disability, racial minorities, or the mentally ill? Is it right for people in these groups to face capital punishment? These and many other questions will be discussed in the following chapters.

 ## Text-Dependent Questions

1. In how many US states is the death penalty legal? How many consider it illegal? How many states have ended capital punishment temporarily?
2. What factors influence whether or not an offense is judged to be a crime worthy of the death penalty?

 ## Research Project

Using the Internet or your school library, research the topic of capital punishment and the criminal justice system, and answer the following question: "Can a government's criminal justice system be trusted to administer capital punishment correctly?" You'll find that some people claim that with human systems, there will always be some amount of error, but the criminal justice system has many standards, such as "innocent until proven guilty" and the right to appeal, that make the correct decision most likely, even if it is capital punishment. Others contend that there is discrimination in courts as well as varying skill levels of attorneys that can unjustly affect the outcome of a capital case. When someone's life is at stake, we cannot trust the criminal justice system to be correct. Write a two-page report, using data you have found in your research to support your conclusion, and present it to your class.

The Origins of
Capital Punishment

Throughout history, governments have executed those it considers to be criminals. Some of the earliest societies believed that a government had the right to take revenge on behalf of a victim. This right was laid down in an ancient legal principle known as *lex talionis* ("law of retaliation"), which says "an eye for an eye, a tooth for a tooth, a life for a life."

The principle of *lex talionis* appears as far back as the 18th century BCE in the law code of Hammurabi, king of the Babylonians. Under this code, the death penalty was imposed for 25 different crimes. It also appears in Mosaic law, the code of the Hebrew prophet and law-giver Moses, who lived around the 13th century BCE. Mosaic law, which is recorded in the first five books of the Bible, was regarded as the law of God. It

The gas chamber at the Missouri State Penitentiary in St. Louis was used for forty executions between 1937 and 1989. It replaced the previous system of public hangings for those convicted of capital offenses.

The law of Moses, found in the Bible, required death sentences for people who committed certain crimes.

included execution as a punishment for certain crimes against other people or offenses against God.

During In the seventh century BCE, another very harsh law code was imposed by an ancient Greek ruler and lawgiver Draco. Contrary to *lex talionis*, Draco insisted that a whole range of crimes could be punishable by death, including treason, arson, and rape. Today, the word *draconian* is used to describe any harsh law.

In Europe during the early Middle Ages (400 to 1100 CE), the punishment of thieves

 Words to Understand in This Chapter

apostasy—abandonment of a religious faith.

blasphemy—great disrespect shown to God or to something holy.

disembowel—to take the stomach, intestines, etc., out of an animal or person.

draconian—very severe or cruel.

embezzlement—to steal money that one has been trusted with.

heresy—a belief or opinion that does not agree with the official belief or opinion of a particular religion.

retroactively—extending in scope or effect to a prior time.

This stone carving depicts the ancient Mesopotamian ruler Hammurabi, along with part of his legal code. During Hammurabi's reign, the death penalty was used for crimes such as telling lies, stealing from a temple, and even associating with criminals.

and murderers was left to the family of the victim to decide. By the 1100s, people began to believe that serious crimes, such as robbery and murder, were not merely a matter for the victim but were crimes against society as a whole. This belief led to the executions of many criminals in public, so citizens could see that punishment was being carried out and justice done.

In the 15th and 16th centuries, Europeans became divided along religious lines due to the Protestant Reformation, and executions for *heresy* became commonplace. During the reign of Henry VIII of England (1509–1547), for example, an estimated 72,000 people were executed, many of them for "religious crimes." European settlers who moved to the New World brought the idea of the death penalty with them. Laws regarding the death penalty varied from one American colony to

In medieval times, public hangings drew large crowds, including families with children. Multiple hangings were common: the gallows at Tyburn in London could hang eight criminals at once.

another and, after the formation of the US, from one state to another.

Capital punishment remained widespread throughout the world until the 19th century, when, in Western Europe and in some US states, it began to be replaced by other kinds of punishment, such as life imprisonment. The death penalty was reintroduced in the 20th century by authoritarian regimes such as Nazi Germany and Fascist Italy.

Today there is a global trend away from capital punishment. By 2014, it had been abolished in two-thirds of all countries, with 98 countries being abolitionist for all crimes, seven

In China, criminals were often executed by having their heads cut off with a sword in a public square.

abolitionist for ordinary crimes (not for special circumstances like military crimes), and 35 abolitionist in practice (the death penalty is legal, but no executions have been carried out for at least a decade). Fifty-eight countries still retain and administer the death penalty for ordinary crimes.

How Were People Executed in the Past?

The human imagination can be seen at its most cruel in the methods devised for executing criminals. Whereas in recent times, there has been a conscious effort to make the process of administering death relatively quick and painless, earlier societies appeared to take delight in inventing methods that could be painful and gruesome. Such methods included criminals being stoned to death, burned alive, fed to wild animals, or ripped apart after being tied to horses that were running in opposite directions.

 Iron Age Executions

The Roman historian Tacitus (56–c. 120 CE) tells of the punishments for crimes among the Iron Age tribes in Germany: "The mode of execution varies according to the offense. Traitors and deserters are hanged in trees; cowards, shirkers . . . are pressed down under a wicker hurdle into the slimy mud of a bog . . . offenders against the state should be made a public example of, whereas deeds of shame should be buried out of men's sight."

In ancient Rome, murderers and traitors were hurled from a clifftop near the city known as the Tarpeian Rock. Those who killed their fathers were drowned in a sealed bag together with a dog, a cock, an ape, and a viper.

Another form of execution in the ancient world was impalement, or driving a stake through a person's body and leaving the person to hang there dying a horrible death. Crucifixion, in which a person was nailed to a stake or a cross, was a variation on this. Most people think of the Romans when they think of crucifixion, but this practice was done by many ancient civilizations. Crucifixion probably originated with the Persians, and there are records of crucifixion being carried out by the ancient Assyrians, Scythians, Carthaginians, Germans,

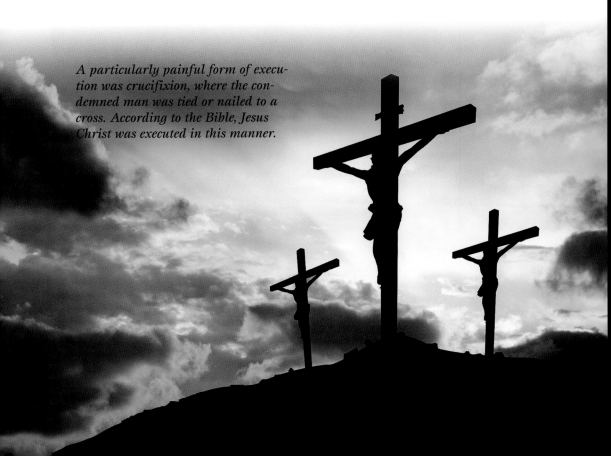

A particularly painful form of execution was crucifixion, where the condemned man was tied or nailed to a cross. According to the Bible, Jesus Christ was executed in this manner.

Celts, and Britons. Some of these references date back to 500 BCE or earlier.

Cruel forms of execution in ancient China included sawing the condemned in half or boiling them in oil. In Europe, offenders were sometimes hanged, drawn, and quartered:

In many places, including medieval Europe and colonial America, those accused of witch-craft or sorcery were often burned alive.

hanged criminals were taken down from the scaffold while still alive, *disemboweled*, and forced to watch their entrails being burned in front of them. They were then beheaded and their bodies chopped into four pieces.

Where Were Executions Held?

In ancient cultures, executions were always carried out in very busy, public settings. There were two two reasons for this. The authorities wanted to inflict the greatest amount of physical torment and shame on the criminal. More importantly, they wanted to deter others from committing such crimes. A Roman leader named Quintilian, who lived around the time of Jesus Christ in the first century CE, wrote, "Whenever we crucify the guilty, the most crowded roads are chosen, where the most people can see and be moved by this fear."

Until relatively recently, in many countries executions were seen as public events and were often attended by large crowds. Public executions were banned in England in 1868 but continued to take place in parts of the United States until the 1930s. In Guatemala, executions have even been broadcast on television.

 "The commandment 'Thou shall not kill' has absolute value and concerns both the innocent and the guilty . . . Even criminals maintain the inviolable right to life, the gift of God."

—Roman Catholic Pope Francis, February 2016

Attitudes toward public executions began to change during the eighteenth century, when more "humane" methods of execution were sought. During the French Revolution at the end of the eighteenth century, for example, the guillotine was developed. It was a mechanical beheading device that proved far more quick and efficient than the traditional executioner's axe. In 1890, the electric chair was used for the first time in New York state, and other states soon adopted this method, which was viewed as less cruel than hanging. In 1924, cyanide gas

French soldiers guard convicts who have been called out to witness an execution by guillotine. The device was considered more "humane" because the execution was swifter and believed to be less painful than hanging or other forms of capital punishment used prior to its invention.

In the 1920s gas chambers, such as this one in Wyoming, began to be used for executions. However, amid evidence that they caused a slow and painful death the chambers were gradually taken out of use. The last execution in the United States that utilized a gas chamber occurred in 1992 in Arizona. Today, most states that have the death penalty proscribe lethal injection as the means for execution, although a few states allow use of the gas chamber as a secondary method of execution.

was introduced in Nevada as a more humane form of execution, and in 1977, Oklahoma became the first state to adopt lethal injection.

Traditional methods of execution, such as beheading and stoning, still persist in some countries around the world, including Saudi Arabia, Iran, Sudan, and Nigeria. Public executions continue to be carried out in some 20 countries although the practice has been condemned by the United Nations Human Rights Committee as "incompatible with human dignity."

Why Are People Executed?

Capital punishment is usually reserved for the most serious offenses, but what is a serious offense? In most countries, the worst crime of all is considered to be murder, and all countries with the death penalty execute murderers. Some countries also regard terrorism, drug dealing, rape, and *blasphemy* against their deity or religious beliefs as offenses worthy of the death penalty.

 "I believe there are some crimes—mass murder, the rape and murder of a child—so heinous that the community is justified in expressing the full measure of its outrage by meting out the ultimate punishment."

—Barack Obama, *The Audacity of Hope* (2006)

What is or is not a capital crime depends very much on the type of government and the culture and traditions of a particular country. In Iraq, for example, someone can be executed for kidnapping. In Sri Lanka, the death penalty can be imposed for helping someone commit suicide or for dealing drugs. In Zambia, merely wounding someone in the course of a robbery can lead to capital punishment.

In certain Muslim countries, such as Sudan, Iran, Pakistan, and Saudi Arabia, *apostasy* from Islam and blasphemy are capital offenses. In Egypt and Kuwait—countries that have suffered from terrorist attacks—terrorism carries a death sentence. And in at least 25 countries, financial crimes such as corruption, *embezzlement,* bribery, fraud, forgery, smuggling, and theft are capital offenses.

Some countries impose the death penalty for certain crimes *retroactively.* Israel imposed a death sentence on Nazi war criminal Adolf Eichmann for heinous acts against Jews, even though the crimes he committed had occurred in Europe before the modern state of Israel had even been established. In Nigeria, people have been executed for drug offenses committed before the death penalty had been applied to such crimes.

 # Text-Dependent Questions

1. What were two law codes in which the principle of lex talionis was applied?
2. Name three examples of execution methods that were considered "humane," starting in 18th-century France.

 # Research Project

Using the Internet or your school library, research the topic of crimes punishable by death in the world, and answer the following question: "Should capital punishment be applied for crimes other than murder?" Some believe each country has the right to decide what constitutes a capital crime, according to its own traditions, and it is not for others to judge them. Others argue that people should not be executed for crimes like fighting against unjust regimes or disobeying unjust laws. Similarly, poor people must sometimes steal to survive, and it is not fair that they should die for this. The death penalty should not be applied outside of murder cases. Write a two-page report, using data you have found in your research to support your conclusion, and present it to your class.

3

Debating Capital Punishment

T he issue of capital punishment has stirred fierce debate among philosophers, campaigners, and legal experts. The arguments for and against are both moral and practical. The moral arguments have to do with personal beliefs about the subject. The practical arguments are concerned with how the system works socially, legally, and financially.

Supporters of the death penalty argue that capital punishment is a fair form of vengeance, exacting justice for the victim's relatives and society in general while reinforcing the moral code upon which society is based. They believe that a murderer has forfeited the right to his or her own life.

Opponents of capital punishment say that punishing murderers by killing them sends out the message that killing is not

The electric chair was a common form of execution in the USA during the twentieth century. Although most states where the death penalty is legal have replaced execution with lethal injection, a few states—including Alabama, Florida, South Carolina, and Virginia—still allow prisoners to choose this form of execution.

always wrong. Death penalty supporters reject this argument: if capital punishment teaches people to kill, they say, do prison sentences teach people that it is okay to hold someone against their will? Do fines teach that it is all right to steal? They say that this argument confuses killing the innocent with punishing the guilty.

Those who wish to officially end the death penalty, known as *abolitionists*, believe that all people have a right to life, but capital punishment violates this right in an inhuman and degrading manner. In answer to this, Ed Koch, former mayor of New York City and supporter of the death penalty, said, "It is by exacting the highest penalty for the taking of human life that we affirm the highest value of life."

Aside from the moral issues, there is also a debate about how well the death penalty works in practice. Is it possible to administer a system of capital punishment in a way that is just and fair? How can we ensure that innocent people are not executed? Does capital punishment deter others from committing murder? Does it make society safer? These are all practical questions for which there is not an easy answer.

 Words to Understand in This Chapter

abolitionist—one who seeks to officially end something.
disproportionate—too large or too small in comparison with something else.
moratorium—a time when a particular activity is not allowed.
premeditated—planned in advance.

Anti-death penalty protesters demonstrate on the steps of a state courthouse, hoping to win a stay of execution for a convicted criminal.

Religious Views on Capital Punishment?

Historically, both Jews and Christians have justified capital punishment by the Old Testament passage, "Whoever sheds the blood of man, by man shall his blood be shed . . ." (Genesis 9:6). However, there are also passages in the Bible that require the death penalty for actions such as sex before marriage, adultery, homosexuality, and working on the Sabbath (the holy day of the week). Many Jews and Christians today believe that capital punishment in these passages have little relevance in mod-

In a 2015 letter, Pope Francis said that capital punishment "is an offense against the inviolability of life and the dignity of the human person, which contradicts God's plan for man and society, and his merciful justice, and impedes the penalty from fulfilling any just objective. It does not render justice to the victims, but rather fosters vengeance."

ern society because it was specific to the original Old Testament context.

Today, there is no general agreement among Jews or Christians on the morality of capital punishment. During the second half of the 20th century, a number of religious leaders—especially Jews and Roman Catholics—campaigned against the death penalty. Capital punishment was abolished by the Jewish state of Israel for all offenses except treason and crimes against humanity. Both the Roman Catholic popes John Paul II and Pope Benedict XVI condemned the death penalty as "cruel and unnecessary." In February 2016, Pope Francis proposed that world leaders who are Catholic should suspend the practice of

Although the Hebrew Bible required the death sentence for certain crimes, over centuries Jewish scholars have restricted the cases in which a death sentence is imposed. In the modern state of Israel, only two convicted criminals have been executed. One was Meir Tobianski, a soldier falsely accused of treason in 1948. The other was Adolf Eichmann, a Nazi official who had been in charge of deporting more than 5 million Jews to extermination camps during the Holocaust. After a public trial, Eichmann was hanged in Jerusalem in 1962.

Dictator Saddam Hussein is pictured sitting before an Iraqi judge in a courtroom in Baghdad. During the 1980s and 1990s, Saddam committed terrible crimes against his country's Kurdish and Shiite Muslim citizens. In 2006, one day after being convicted by a special tribunal, Saddam was hanged for his crimes. Many people were appalled that the sentence had been carried out so quickly.

capital punishment for a year, while working toward permanently ending criminal executions altogether.

Muslims follow Islamic law, known as *Sharia*, which is based on teaching of the Muslim holy book, the Qur'an. *Sharia* defines how believers should behave, and it also lays down suitable punishments for offenses. Death is the accepted punishment for several *hudud* crimes (infractions that have fixed penalties in the Qur'an). In Islamic countries such as Saudi

Arabia and Sudan, *Sharia* is enshrined in the nation's laws, and cases are tried in *Sharia* courts.

Two other major world religions, Hinduism and Buddhism, do not explicitly forbid the death penalty; however, in these religions the sanctity of life is predominant so that the death penalty is rarely, if ever, used. People in Buddhist countries like Japan tend to be opposed to the death penalty. India, a predominantly Hindu nation, permits death sentences in certain extreme cases, but these are relatively rare. As of 2016, there

In January 2016, hundreds of people gathered in New York's Times Square to protest the Saudi government's execution of a dissident Shiite cleric, Nimr Baqir al-Nimr, and to demand the release of other prisoners. The 2016 execution of al-Nimr and 46 other Saudi prisoners increased tensions between Saudi Arabia, where Sunni Islam is the official religion, and neighboring Iran, where most of the residents are Shiite Muslims.

were about 100 people on death row in India, a nation of nearly 1.3 billion people.

What about the Rights of Victims?

In the United States, some family members choose to attend the execution of their relative's murderer. This may help to bring a sense of closure to their suffering. Justice for victims is often given as a major justification for the death penalty.

> "To take a life when a life has been lost is revenge, not justice."
>
> —South African Archbishop Desmond Tutu,

In general, many families of murder victims believe that their feelings, as well as the rights of their dead relative, wind up being overlooked in the general debate over how the killer should be punished. In the US, several groups have been formed by relatives of murder victims, including Justice for All and Citizens against Homicide. These groups offer families support and advice on how to obtain compensation for their loss, for example, and how to campaign to keep the murderer of their relative in prison.

Some victims' families do not support capital punishment. They may express a wish that their loss should not be used as a reason for another family's bereavement. Others have said that execution is too quick and easy a punishment and believe that life imprisonment will give the murderer more time to think about his or her actions. Still others have expressed forgiveness for the murderer. One American victim group, Murder Victims' Families for Reconciliation (MVFR), actively campaigns against the death penalty with the mission statement, "Our opposition to the death penalty is rooted in our direct experience of loss and our refusal to respond to that loss with a quest for more killing. Executions are not what will help us heal."

In Islamic countries, the families of murder victims often get to decide on the punishment of their relative's killer. According to *Sharia* law, murder is not a *hudud* crime, meaning that it does not carry a fixed penalty as laid down in the Qur'an. The penalty for *premeditated* murder given by *Sharia* courts is usually death, but it is up to the victim's family to decide whether the sentence is carried out or not. They may ask for *qisas*, or retaliation, which means death for a convicted murderer, or they may choose to pardon the murderer and accept "blood money"— financial compensation for the loss—called *diya*.

Sister Helen Prejean, a campaigner against the death penalty, wrote the influential book Dead Man Walking *(1994), which opened many people's eyes to the dreadful existence of prisoners on death row.*

The Qur'an encourages victims' families to choose *diya*, promising the forgiveness of sins to those who extend forgiveness to murderers. Executions may be delayed for many years if, for example, the heirs of a victim are not yet old enough to make their decision. *Diya* can sometimes take place on the very day of execution. In June 2001, a 20-year-old Yemeni man's life was spared by the victim's father just as the executioner was raising his sword to behead him.

Bias and Capital Punishment

It has been claimed that the implementation of the death penalty is unfair to people with low incomes. Poor people make up the vast majority of prisoners on death row in the United States. They often cannot afford to hire their own lawyers and must depend on public defenders of varying quality. In some states, such as Alabama, there is no public defender system, and the court will assign an attorney to low-income defendants from a pool of local lawyers. These lawyers are usually poorly paid and often lack any significant experience in capital punishment cases, which may lead to a failure to call important witnesses or to present evidence that could mean the difference between life and death for a defendant.

Sometimes, racial prejudice can be a factor motivating juries on capital cases, leading to the execution of ethnic

 US Executions by Race

Death row inmates executed in the United States between January 1976 and January 2016:

Race of Defendant	Number Executed	% of Total
White	787	55.4%
Black	492	34.6%
Latino	118	8.3%
Other	24	1.7%

Source: Bureau of Justice Statistics.

Sister Helen Prejean, a Roman Catholic nun who has been a leading advocate for abolishing the death penalty, has said, "The death penalty is a poor person's issue. Always remember that: after all the rhetoric that goes on in the legislative assemblies, in the end . . . it is the poor who are selected to die in this country."

minorities in *disproportionate* numbers. A 2007 study of death sentences in Connecticut conducted by Yale University School of Law revealed that African-American defendants receive the death penalty at three times the rate of white defendants in cases where the victims are white. Research in the US has shown that in capital cases where the defendant was black and the victim was white, conviction rates varied according to the racial makeup of the jury. When there were four or fewer

In recent years, the Black Lives Matter protest movement has drawn attention to the issue of racial profiling among police officers and of bias in the criminal justice system.

white males on the jury in a case, 30 percent of juries opted for the death penalty. But when there were five or more white men on the jury, 70 percent sentenced the defendant to death. Evidence also suggests that sentences vary according to the ethnicity of the victim. 77 percent of prisoners executed in the US since 1977 were convicted of killing a white victim, even though only about half of murder victims were white.

By the same token, some people point to a discrepancy in the conviction rates between the sexes. In 2014, there were just 57 women on death row in the United States, making up a mere 1.9 percent of the total number of prisoners awaiting execution. Since 1976, only 15 women have been executed in the US, compared with 1,374 men. Certain countries even exclude women from the death penalty. These include Belarus, Mongolia, Uzbekistan, Cuba, and Russia. However, death penalty supporters argue that it is unfair to treat convicted criminals differently on the basis of gender.

The Execution of Innocent People

Criminal justice systems sometimes make mistakes, and there are many cases of people convicted of crimes who have later been proven innocent. One famous example is the case of the Birmingham Six, a group of six men who spent 16 years in prison in the United Kingdom after being charged with causing a bomb explosion in 1974. They were later freed when evidence used against them in the trial was discredited. People who have spent time in prison for crimes they did not commit are justifiably angry about their ordeal. It is even more impactful when innocent people are wrongly accused and executed.

Misadministration of justice is most likely to occur when there is government or media pressure on the police and justice system to find and convict an offender. This might happen following a particularly notorious crime that has aroused a lot of public anger. Or it might happen after a government crackdown, such as the "war on crime" in Russia from 1995 to 1996. During this period, the rate of people executed who were later found to be innocent was 30 percent, up from the 15 percent rate before the "war on crime."

The Appeal System

In the US, 3,194 people out of 8,466 (37.8 percent) were released from death row between 1976 and 2013, many because new evidence had emerged to prove their innocence. Supporters of the death penalty argue that these figures show that the appeals process works, and the innocent are generally saved from execution in a system that properly administers justice. However, many of these cases were overturned not because of the appeals process, but thanks to confessions by other criminals, the application of new scientific techniques to old evidence, and the efforts of campaigners working outside the justice system.

Other death-penalty supporters cast doubt on the statistics. They say there should be a distinction made between "legal innocence" and "actual innocence." They claim the figure of 3,194 prisoners released includes many whose guilty verdict was overturned simply due to a legal technicality, not because they were actually innocent of the crime.

It is very difficult to calculate how many innocent people in

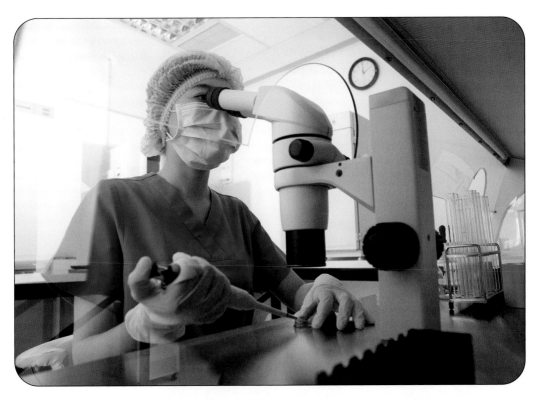

Samples of human DNA can be lifted from hair, skin, blood or saliva and they can be compared to other samples found at a crime scene.

the United States may have been executed because US courts do not generally review cases once a defendant is dead. However, there are several examples of executed people with strong claims of innocence. The development of DNA testing has thrown the legitimacy of several convictions into doubt. In 2016, the Death Penalty Information Center published a list of 10 inmates that it deemed "executed but possibly innocent."

DNA Testing

DNA testing is a method of identifying a person by analyzing

Kirk Bloodsworth, the first person to be sentenced to death and then subsequently exonerated, speaks during the launch of the book, Moving Away from the Death Penalty: Arguments, Trends and Perspectives *in November 2015.*

their DNA, a molecule found in every cell of every living organism that is unique to that individual. There is a campaign in the US to make DNA testing available to all death-row inmates who are claiming innocence. In 2011, 48 states passed laws to allow this to happen, including all 34 states that employ capital punishment. The extent to which DNA testing is allowed varies by state. By removing any doubt from a conviction, DNA testing could rob abolitionists of one of their key arguments against the death penalty: the possibility of innocence.

The first Death Row convict exonerated by DNA testing was Kirk Bloodsworth, who had been convicted in 1985 of the rape and murder of a young girl. The science of DNA testing was just developing in the early 1990s, and Bloodsworth asked for it to be applied to the prosecutor's evidence in his case. The testing showed that he had not committed the murder and he was released from prison in 1993. By that time he had spent nine years in prison, including two on Maryland's death row.

Similarly, Ray Krone spent ten years in prison in Arizona after being convicted of the murder of a bartender in 1991. In 2002, he became the one-hundredth death row inmate to be exonerated by DNA testing.

Fair Trials

One way of reducing the number of executions of innocent people is to ensure that the criminal justice system observes the rights of the defendant to a fair trial. The United Nations, a global organization of countries formed after World War II, has sought to establish a set of legal standards that all countries with the death penalty should abide by. These include the following: defendants should be informed of the nature of the charge against them and be given enough time to prepare a defense; defendants should be given adequate legal representation as well as access to examine witnesses to help their case; they should expect a fair trial with an unbiased jury; and have the right to appeal against the verdict.

Many countries with the death penalty fall far short of these standards. In Saudi Arabia, trials have taken place in which the defendant has no legal representation at all. The right to prepare a defense, to a fair trial, and to appeal have all been denied on many occasions in China, where executions have sometimes been carried out between six and eight days after an arrest. In Iran, there have been reports of drug offenders being refused both legal representation and the right of appeal.

Is the Death Penalty a Deterrent?

One of the major arguments in favor of capital punishment is that it deters other criminals. It is believed that people will be less likely to commit murder if they know that they may be sentenced to death themselves when they are caught. However, abolitionists reject the deterrence argument. They claim that most murders are not planned in advance by rational people who consider the consequences of their actions. Murderers are often people who have found it difficult to fit into normal society. Their crimes are usually the result of thoughtless outbursts of anger or fear. Death-penalty supporters counter that the low number of rational, calculating killers is perhaps explained by the presence of the death penalty.

John McAdams of the Marquette University Department of Political Science said, "If we execute murderers, and there is in fact no deterrent effect, we have killed a bunch of murderers. If we fail to execute murderers, and doing so would in fact have deterred other murders, we have allowed the killing of a bunch of innocent victims. I would much rather risk the former. This, to me, is not a tough call."

Statistical evidence has been used both for and against the deterrence argument. Death-penalty supporters point to the dramatic rise in murders in the US during and just after the period 1967-1976, when there was a national *moratorium* on

In some US prisons, death row inmates spend up to 23 hours alone in their cells. They leave their cells to shower (often handcuffed) and to exercise in a restricted area often called a "recreation cage."

executions. Between 1966 and 1980, executions in the US averaged less than one every four years, and the murder rate nearly doubled, from 5.6 to 10.2 per 100,000 people. From 1995 to 2000, US executions rose to 71 per year, and by 1999, the murder rate had fallen to 5.7 per 100,000, its lowest level since 1966.

There are also instances in which the murder rate has not risen after a country has abolished the death penalty. In some cases, the murder rate has actually fallen. Capital punishment was abolished in Canada in 1976 and the rate of murders per

100,000 citizens dropped from 3.09 in 1975 to 1.44 in 2013.

Some capital-punishment supporters completely reject the deterrence argument, contending that the death penalty should simply punish the guilty and not be used as an example to society. They say that the deterrence argument would be a very unfair reason to support the death penalty since it implies that people are killed, not because they deserve it, but for the good of society. As the Christian writer C.S. Lewis explained, "If deterrence is all that matters, the execution of an innocent man, provided the public think him guilty, would be fully justified."

Another obvious point often made by death-penalty supporters is that an executed killer cannot one day escape from prison or be set free, enabling that person to kill or injure again. Therefore, they say, capital punishment contributes to the safety of our society. However, statistics show that it is generally very rare for murderers to kill again if they are released from prison. In her 2012 book *Life After Murder*, Nancy Mullane documented 988 convicted murderers who were released from prisons in California over a twenty-year period. Of those murderers, 1 percent were arrested for committing new crimes, and 10 percent were arrested for violating parole. None were re-arrested for murder over the period she examined.

What Is the Cost of the Death Penalty?

On the face of it, the death penalty would appear to be a way of saving the taxpaying public the cost of keeping someone in prison for life. After a person is executed, there are no further costs to the state. However, research has shown that, in the US at least, the death penalty system is actually more expensive to administer than life imprisonment. This is because of the combined costs of funding appeals and keeping death-row inmates in prison for years, even decades, while the appeals process takes place. A 2003 study showed that each death penalty case in Texas cost taxpayers about $2.3 million more than a case resulting in life imprisonment without parole.

 # Text-Dependent Questions

1. Explain how capital punishment can be carried out unfairly based on the defendant's class, race, or gender.
2. What defendants' rights does the UN recommend in order to help ensure a fair trial for someone who might face the death penalty?

 # Research Project

Using the Internet or your school library, research the topic of capital punishment and victims' families, and answer the following question: "In murder cases, should the wishes of the victim's family be considered when administering a sentence on a capital crime?" Some think that since the victim's family is most affected by the crime, family members should have a say in the punishment of the murderer. Others say the government needs consistency in giving punishments for crimes, and if family members affect the sentence, the government will not be fair and impartial to criminals. Write a two-page report, using data you have found in your research to support your conclusion, and present it to your class.

4

The Movement to Abolish Capital Punishment

T he modern movement to abolish capital punishment dates back to the 18th century. In 1764, the Italian scholar Cesare Beccaria published *On Crimes and Punishments*, which proposed the abolition of the death penalty. Beccaria believed that it was inhumane and ineffective and that it gave legitimacy to killing: "It seems to me absurd that the laws, which are an expression of the public will, which detest and punish homicide, should themselves commit it, and that to deter citizens from murder they order a public one."

In the 1780s, Beccaria's ideas were taken up by the rulers of Russia, Austria, and Tuscany, where capital punishment was suspended for several years. The abolitionist movement grew in Europe and the United States, and in 1794, Pennsylvania became the first state in the US to abolish capital

A police officer uncovers a drug smuggler's hiding place inside of a spare tire. Today, 32 countries allow the death penalty for people found guilty of drug smuggling.

punishment for all crimes but murder. In 1861, Michigan became the first US state—and the first territory anywhere in the world—to abolish capital punishment for all crimes. It was soon followed by Rhode Island and Wisconsin. In 1863, Venezuela became the first country to abolish capital punishment for all crimes.

European states soon began to follow this example. In 1861, England abandoned capital punishment for all crimes except murder, and by 1925, Portugal, the Netherlands, Norway, Sweden, Italy, Romania, Austria, and Switzerland had abolished the death penalty for all peacetime crimes. A similar movement occurred among several newly independent South American states, including Brazil, Colombia, Uruguay, and Argentina.

However, the movement towards abolition was not a one-way process. Many European and South American countries fell under authoritarian regimes in the 1930s and 1940s, which reimposed capital punishment. By 1965, 25 countries had abolished the death penalty for murder, and 11 of these had abolished it for all crimes.

 Words to Understand in This Chapter

extradition—the surrender of an alleged criminal by one authority (as a state) to another authority having to try the charged criminal.

ratify—to make a policy official by signing it or voting for it.

It is estimated that 20,000 people turned out to witness the hanging of Rainey Bertha in Kentucky in June 1936. Newspapers from across the nation came to report on the spectacle. The ensuing media circus led to the abolishment of all public executions in Kentucky two years later. This event also represented the last official public hanging in the United States.

Abolitionist Countries

Between 1965 and 2014, the number of abolitionist countries grew from 25 to 105 (98 for all crimes, seven for ordinary crimes only). A further 35 countries have not executed anyone for a number of years and are regarded as abolitionist in practice. In 1965, there were two abolitionist countries outside Europe and Central and South America. By 2014, 18 countries

Sergei Ordzhonikidze, Director-General of the United Nations Office at Geneva (UNOG), addresses the opening session of the three-day Fourth World Congress Against the Death Penalty, hosted by UNOG and the National Council of Switzerland in 2010.

from Africa were on the list as well as another 20 from the Asia-Pacific region.

There have been a few formerly abolitionist countries that have brought back capital punishment, including Papua New Guinea (abolished in 1975 and reinstated in 1991) and the Philippines (abolished in 1987, reinstated in 1993, and abolished again in 2006). Nevertheless, the worldwide trend remains in the direction of abolition.

Is the United Nations against Capital Punishment?

During the second half of the 20th century, there was a remarkable increase in the number of abolitionist countries. One of the main reasons for this was the success of abolitionists in making capital punishment an international human rights issue rather than a matter for each country to decide on for themselves.

The process began with the "Universal Declaration of Human Rights," passed by the UN in 1948. Although this did not specifically condemn capital punishment, it did contain several clauses that could be interpreted as being against the death penalty. Article Three affirmed that everyone has a right to life, and Article Five declared that no one should face "cruel, inhuman, or degrading . . . punishment." This marked a turning point in the attitudes of many governments; of the 98 countries that were abolitionist for all crimes in 2014, 84 abolished the death penalty after 1948.

In 1966, the UN adopted an agreement called the International Covenant on Civil and Political Rights (ICCPR).

Again, capital punishment was not specifically banned, but it did proclaim that "every human being has the right to life" and that "no one shall be arbitrarily deprived of his life." Article six of the ICCPR said that capital punishment should be restricted to "the most serious of crimes."

In 1971, the UN took its first step toward declaring the abolition of the death penalty as a universal goal. The organization passed a resolution calling for a restriction in the number of crimes for which the death penalty could be imposed, with the aim of eventual abolition of capital punishment.

The UN passed a further resolution in 1989 requiring sig-

 ## Extradition Cases

Extradition is the handing over, by a government, of somebody accused of a crime in a different country for trial and punishment there. In 1989, the European Court of Human Rights prohibited the extradition of a suspect accused of a capital offense to the US state of Virginia. The court decided he would face "inhuman/degrading treatment or punishment," which went against the European Convention on Human Rights. This developed into a firm policy of the European Union in 2000.

Since 2001, many other countries, including Canada, Mexico, and South Africa have also refused to extradite wanted criminals to the United States unless they receive assurances from American prosecutors that they will not seek the death penalty.

American soldiers search for terrorists during a 2006 patrol in Taji, Iraq. Some countries have refused to hand suspected terrorists over to the United States because Americans will not rule out the possibility of capital sentences for them.

natories to abolish capital punishment, except in times of war, and banning any state from re-establishing the death penalty after having abolished it. By 2014, a total of 81 countries had ratified this agreement. Three other countries had signed the agreement but not yet ratified it.

Have Any Countries Refused to Sign?

One of the main obstacles faced by those who wish to impose a universal ban on capital punishment is that many countries

Egyptian police investigate a car bomb that was intended to kill the country's Minister of the Interior in Cairo, 2013. The Egyptian government has imposed the death penalty for many forms of terrorism.

see it as an attempt by the international community to interfere with their own internal laws and customs. Countries such as Egypt, Singapore, and Saudi Arabia have regularly refused to sign UN resolutions on the death penalty or introduced amendments to them that preserved the rights of individual countries to choose their own justice systems without outside interference.

In 2000, the US government replied to a UN survey with the following statement, advocating for the right to choose:

"We recognize that many countries have abolished the death penalty under their domestic laws and that a number of countries have accepted treaty obligations to that effect, and we respect their decision to do so. However, we believe that in democratic societies the criminal justice system . . . should reflect the will of the people freely expressed and appropriately implemented through their elected representatives."

Organizations Against Capital Punishment

The Council of Europe—an organization of European countries that seeks to protect human rights—was inspired by the UN's 1971 call to abolish the death penalty. In 1982, it adopted a resolution requiring the abolition of capital punishment in peacetime. By 2015, this had been ratified by 46 countries out of 47, with Russia being the only one that signed the resolution but did not formally *ratify* it.

In early 2003, the Council of Europe took the final step towards complete abolition. An agreement was passed that the death penalty should be banned in all circumstances, both during war and peacetime. By 2015, this agreement had been ratified by 44 countries, signed but not ratified by one, and not signed by two.

"The American people have determined that the good to be derived from capital punishment in deterrence and perhaps most of all in the meting out of condign justice for horrible crimes—outweighs the risk of error."

—U.S. Supreme Court Justice Antonin Scalia

Headquarters of the Council of Europe, which has passed resolutions to abolish the application of the death penalty in peacetime.

The Council of Europe's stand had a powerful effect on countries in Central and Eastern Europe hoping to join the European Union (EU). The Council established as a condition of their membership that they suspend executions and move towards complete abolition. This prompted several—including the Czech Republic, Hungary, Romania, Slovakia, and Slovenia—to abolish the death penalty and has led to problems for Turkey, which has tried to become a member.

The Organization of American States (OAS)—an organization of countries in North and South America—adopted an agreement in 1990 that called on states to abstain from using the death penalty. However, it did not insist that they repeal the laws permitting its use. By 2015, 13 countries, all from South and Central America, had ratified the agreement.

 # Text-Dependent Questions

1. What two early documents/policies did the UN draft that eventually led to its goal of universal abolition of the death penalty?
2. What was the stance of the US on UN resolutions to ban the death penalty?

 # Research Project

Using the Internet or your school library, research the topic of capital punishment and extradition, and answer the following question: "Should a country have to send its own citizen back to another country where he or she committed a capital crime, even though the offender may face the death penalty?"

Some contend the offender's country of origin is responsible for its citizens and should protect them. One government does not have the right to execute someone from another country, so the country of origin should not have to send its citizen back to the country where a capital offense took place.

Others argue that a country has the right to try and, if necessary, execute someone who breaks its laws, whatever their nation of origin, since the crime was committed in that country. Otherwise the victims of the crime would be unable to see punishment delivered according to their justice system.

Write a two-page report, using data you have found in your research to support your conclusion, and present it to your class.

5

Do Vulnerable People Get Executed?

Many people have argued that there are certain populations that should not be subjected to the death penalty. These include young people, elderly people, pregnant women, new mothers, those with mental illness, people with intellectual disabilities, and foreign nationals.

Some believe that all murders should be punishable by death, and that the age of the murderer is not relevant. They say that setting a minimum age for those who may face capital punishment would be *arbitrary*. However, many others believe that young people form a separate category because they are less mature, and therefore less responsible, for their actions. They point out that many young murderers are themselves victims of abuse, and they should perhaps be helped rather than executed.

⬅

Most states have considered laws that would exempt criminals from execution if they are deemed to be mentally ill or impaired. To date only Connecticut has passed such a law. That state subsequently banned capital punishment in 2012, rendering the legal protection moot.

The international community is generally in favor of banning the execution of the young. In 1984, the UN passed a resolution stating that persons under 18 years of age at the time a crime was committed should not be sentenced to death. This commitment was confirmed by the Convention of the Rights of the Child, passed by the UN in November 1989, which has been ratified by every member nation except the United States. Since 1990, a number of nations have passed laws banning the execution of young people, including Yemen, China, Sudan, and Thailand. In 2001, Pakistan *commuted* death sentences on nearly 100 juveniles to life imprisonment.

Despite having ratified international treaties banning capital punishment for those under 18 years of age, certain countries continue to execute people who are under 18 or commit-

 Words to Understand in This Chapter

arbitrary—not planned or chosen for a particular reason; not based on reason or evidence.

commute—to change (a punishment) to a less severe one.

consul—a government official whose job is to live in a foreign country and protect and help the citizens of his or her own country who are traveling, living, or doing business there.

migrant—a person who goes from one place to another especially to find work.

prisoner of war—a member of the armed forces of a nation who is taken by the enemy during combat.

senility—showing a loss of mental ability (such as memory) in old age.

subjective—based on feelings or opinions rather than facts.

An accused person talks with his legal counsel. Many countries, such as the United States, Thailand and Turkey, offer free legal representation to defendants who cannot afford a lawyer.

ted crimes when they were under 18. In some cases, the minimum age is fixed as low as 16. In Malaysia, there is no legal distinction made between adults and minors, and people under even 16 can be executed. In India, a boy who was 15 at the time of the offense was executed in 2001. In countries like Brazil, where poor street children often have no legal proof of age, it is difficult to be sure whether juveniles are being executed or not.

According to Amnesty International, there have been 90 documented executions of child offenders in nine countries since 1990: China, the Democratic Republic of Congo, Iran,

The US Supreme Court has issued a series of rulings that restrict the types of crimes that can result in capital punishment. In Kennedy v. Louisiana *(2008), the Court ruled that states could only impose the death penalty when a crime resulted in the death of the victim, unless it was a crime against the state such as espionage or treason.*

Nigeria, Pakistan, Saudi Arabia, Sudan, the United States, and Yemen. Nineteen of these executions took place in the United States.

Until relatively recently, the minimum age for the death penalty in the United States varied from state to state. In 1988, the US Supreme Court ruled that it was unconstitutional to impose the death penalty on people under the age of 16 at the time of the offense, but it allowed individual state legislatures to rule on cases involving 16- to 18-year-olds. In March 2005, the United States Supreme Court ruled in *Roper v. Simmons* that the death penalty was "cruel and unusual punishment" for anyone under the age of 18, and was therefore prohibited in all states by the US Constitution.

The argument against the death penalty for young people—that they are less responsible for their actions—cannot be easily applied to the elderly, unless it can be proved that a person was suffering from *senility* when he or she committed a capital crime. Nevertheless, the UN has urged its member states to establish a maximum age beyond which people cannot be sentenced to death. Only ten countries have done this. The maximum age is 60 in Guatemala and Mongolia; 63 in Tajikistan; 65 in Belarus, Kazakhstan, and Russia; 70 in Sudan, South Sudan, and Zimbabwe; and 75 in China.

> "All human beings are born free and equal in dignity and rights. They are endowed [born with] reason and conscience and should act toward one another in a spirit of brotherhood."
>
> —Universal Declaration of Human Rights, 1948

Are Pregnant Women or New Mothers Executed?

Pregnant women charged with capital crimes are not automatically excluded from the death penalty in every country of the world. There have been no recent reports of pregnant women

> "I think this country would be much better off if we did not have capital punishment. . . . We cannot ignore the fact that in recent years a disturbing number of inmates on death row have been exonerated."
>
> —John Paul Stevens, former Supreme Court justice

being executed, although a death sentence was imposed on one woman in the Democratic Republic of Congo in 1998.

New mothers are also not generally executed. Some countries wait for the child to be born and weaned before carrying out the sentence. Other countries, such as Kuwait, commute the sentence to life imprisonment. However, 16 countries, including Egypt, Japan, South Korea, and Turkey, have informed the UN that they could not in all cases exempt new mothers from the death penalty. Several set a period, ranging from two months (Egypt) to two years (Yemen) after the baby is born, before the execution can be carried out.

One well-known case involved an unmarried Nigerian woman, Amina Lawal, who became pregnant. She lived in northern Nigeria, where *Sharia* is the basis for all laws, and according to the Qur'an pregnancy outside of marriage is considered to be evidence of adultery, a crime punishable by death. In March 2002, a local Sharia court sentenced Amina to death by stoning. The man named as father of the baby girl denied having sex with Amina and was released. Human rights groups appealed against Amina's sentence. Initially, the *Sharia* court rejected the appeal and upheld Amina's death sentence, but in September 2003 a higher-level Nigerian court overturned the death sentence.

Although Amina Lawal's case attracted national attention, she was actually the second Nigerian woman condemned by a Sharia court to death by stoning for engaging in sex before marriage. The first woman, Safiya Hussaini, also had her sentence overturned on appeal.

Mental Illnesses and Intellectual Disabilities

In all countries that have the death penalty, allowances are made for people who are mentally ill. Many people believe that if someone is unable to control their actions due to mental illness, then he or she should not be held responsible for them. The problem is that the issue is not always black and white; there are many different forms and degrees of mental illness, and judging whether a person should or should not be held responsible for a crime can be *subjective*.

It may depend on a number of factors, including the defendant's mental state at the time they are examined by a psychiatrist, the views of the particular psychiatrist, the attitude of the jury, and the nature of the crime. Situations can become

Intellectual Disability Cases

People with intellectual disability are particularly vulnerable once they have entered the criminal justice system, as they are less likely to understand their rights and may be eager to please their interrogators by confessing. Earl Washington had an IQ of between 57 and 69. He was convicted of raping and murdering a young woman in Culpeper, Virginia, in 1982 on the evidence of a confession he made to police. It is not certain that all members of the jury were aware of how limited he was intellectually. Some 16 years after being sentenced to death, a DNA test proved his innocence. He was pardoned and released from prison in February 2001 after coming, at one point, within nine days of his execution.

A recent case that attracted national attention was that of Cecil Clayton, who was executed in Missouri on March 17, 2015. Clayton was 74 years old and suffered from dementia. He had an IQ of 71 and part of the frontal lobe of his brain had been removed due to an industrial accident in 1972. The frontal lobe is involved in impulse control and social behavior, and after the accident Clayton began experiencing violent impulses and extreme paranoia. He was in and out of mental hospitals over the next twenty years, until 1996 when he killed a police officer who had responded to a domestic dispute at his home. Defense psychiatrists argued that he did not fully understand what he had done or why he was going to be executed. However, the courts deemed that Clayton was competent, and the US Supreme Court refused to grant a stay of execution.

more complicated when psychiatrists appear as witnesses for both the prosecution and the defense, with each presenting a different view of the defendant's mental state.

In many countries, prisoners who become mentally ill after sentencing to death can still face execution, although it is often delayed until they are judged to have recovered. This places psychiatrists in the awkward position of knowing that the successful treatment of a patient may result in his or her execution.

Intellectual disability is characterized by significant limitations in intellectual functioning and adaptive behavior, with an onset before age 18. In most countries, those with intellectual disability are not executed unless they are judged to be able to understand the consequences of their actions. One

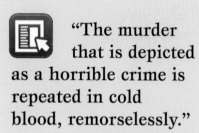

"The murder that is depicted as a horrible crime is repeated in cold blood, remorselessly."

—Cesare Beccaria, *On Crimes and Punishments*

exception is in the US, where 44 prisoners with intellectual disability were executed between 1984 and 2001. In June 2002, the US Supreme Court ruled that executing people with intellectual disability violated the Eighth Amendment to the Constitution, amounting to "cruel and unusual punishment," and it has now been banned throughout the US.

Soldiers and the Death Penalty

Crimes committed by soldiers are usually dealt with in a different way than civilian crimes, especially in wartime. Soldiers are usually tried in military courts and judged by senior officers. In some cases they lack the standard rights and protec-

Some countries use a firing squad in executions. Usually, a team of five or six executioners fire at the prisoner. One of them fires a blank, so the identity of the executioner is not known.

tions granted to civilian defendants. In Uganda in March 2003, three soldiers of the Uganda People's Defense Force were sentenced to death by firing squad for murder. The trial lasted just two days, during which time they had no legal representation. They were given no right to appeal and were executed about an hour after the sentence was passed.

Foreign Nationals

Foreigners accused of capital crimes can be particularly vulnerable if they do not speak or understand the language spoken by their police interrogators or by those who cross-examine them in court. There have been reports that *migrant* workers involved in capital cases in some Middle Eastern countries have not been provided with translations of courtroom proceedings.

> "I have observed that it never does a boy much good to shoot him."
>
> —President Abraham Lincoln, commenting on the case of a soldier sentenced to death for desertion

Under international law, foreign nationals accused of a crime have the right to assistance from a *consul*, a government official from the defendant's country who is based in the country where he or she is being tried. Several foreign nationals have been executed in the US without having been informed of this right, including Karl and Walter LaGrand, German citizens executed for murder in 1999.

Different Rules During Wartime

Many countries that do not have the death penalty in peacetime reserve the right to use it in times of war, when the survival of the country is at stake. The death penalty is seen as a useful means of punishing "enemies of the state," such as spies and saboteurs, and a way of deterring others from these activities. The UN resolutions seeking to ban the death penalty do not apply to wartime situations.

Some governments try to widen the definition of "enemies of the state" to justify executing *prisoners of war*. The Geneva Convention (1949), which has been ratified by almost every UN member state, is concerned with treatment of prisoners of war. In Article Three it prohibits violence or cruel treatment toward prisoners of war. It states that executions can only be carried out after sentencing by a "regularly constituted court affording all the judicial guarantees which are recognized as indispensable by civilized peoples."

Text-Dependent Questions

1. Explain how intellectual disability factored into the capital case of Earl Washington.
2. Are laws regarding capital punishment the same during times of war and peace? Why or why not?

 ## Research Project

Using the Internet or your school library, research the topic of capital punishment and mental illness, and answer the following question: "In capital cases, should criminals with mental illness be treated any differently from other criminals?"

Some believe a person cannot be held responsible, especially for a crime that may entail the death penalty, if they are unable to control their actions. They should be tried and treated differently from criminals who are mentally sound.

Others maintain that what matters is the fact that the crime was committed, not the state of the person's mental health. Because someone was victimized, there needs to be just punishment. Criminals should all be treated the same, whether or not that includes the death penalty.

Write a two-page report, using data you have found in your research to support your conclusion, and present it to your class.

Life on Death Row

Waiting to be executed is a stressful experience. Psychological studies carried out on death row prisoners have shown high levels of frustration, fear, and loneliness that are similar to the feelings experienced by the terminally ill. But for death row prisoners, the effects are made even worse by the often severe conditions they live in.

Prisoners might have to spend a long time waiting to be executed. Because of the length of the appeals process in the US, the period between sentencing and execution can take many years. Gary Graham, the accused murderer whose story was told in the first chapter of this book, had to wait 19 years to be executed for a crime he allegedly committed when he was 17 years old. It is not only the prisoners who suffer, but also their

Cells on Death Row at the Florida State Prison. As of February 2016 there were 389 inmates awaiting execution on Florida's Death Row, including five women. Some of the inmates have been waiting on Death Row since the late 1970s.

families, who may find it hard to remain positive and support-
ive over such long periods. Sometimes the families of victims
also suffer, as they must participate in many legal proceedings
and are unable to achieve a sense of closure for their own
bereavement until the killer of their loved one has finally been
executed.

Prisoners in other countries can also face long delays before
execution. In Saudi Arabia, those convicted of murder must
often wait until the victim's son has reached maturity, which
can be up to 15 years, before their fate is known.

In Malaysia, one man had to wait from 1988 to 2000 before
being executed, while in Zambia, prisoners can live under sentence of death for up to 25 years. However, the country with
the record for keeping prisoners on death row the longest is
Japan, where some prisoners have been waiting for over 30
years to be executed. In Japan, Belarus, and Taiwan, the wait
is made harder to bear because prisoners are not told exactly
when they will be executed.

 Words to Understand in This Chapter

bereavement—the state of being sad because a family member or friend has
recently died.

clemency—kind or merciful treatment of someone who could be given harsh punishment.

jurisdiction—the power, right, or authority to interpret and apply the law.

manacles—a set of metal rings designed to lock around a person's wrists or
ankles.

(Left) Serial killer Ted Bundy spent more than a decade on Florida's death row before being executed in 1989. (Above) Many people celebrated Bundy's execution in the electric chair. This car, parked across the street from a house where Bundy had murdered two students, was photographed on the morning of his execution.

Is There a Right of Appeal?

Under international law, all prisoners sentenced to death have the right to appeal against their sentence to a court of higher *jurisdiction*. Almost all countries claim to observe this right, with the exception of the Revolutionary Courts in Iran and Libya, as well as military courts in several African countries.

Most countries that retain the death penalty offer a fixed period between sentencing and execution for appeals to be lodged. This period varies from country to country. In Madagascar and Chad, for example, it is just three days. Bangladesh allows a week. In China the appeal period is ten days; while in Bahrain, Lesotho, Syria, and Thailand, it is 30 days or more. In the state of Texas, defendants have 30 days following their conviction to present new evidence in their defense, otherwise they lose their right of appeal.

Thus, although most countries offer the right of appeal, in many cases this is not very beneficial since the defendant's lawyers are not given enough time to search for and present new evidence in defense of their client. Three, or even 30, days is not much time to hunt for other witnesses or to locate physical evidence in support of a case.

Sometimes, states will refuse to allow time for appeals. For example, in 1994 a Nigerian human rights activist named Ken Saro-Wiwa was arrested and held without charge for nine months before facing trial for the murder of four Ogoni leaders. Saro-Wiwa had been campaigning on behalf of the Ogoni people, and several human rights groups claimed these were false charges. In October 1995 he was sentenced to death by a military court. He was given no right of appeal and was hanged just ten days later despite worldwide protests.

Do People with Death Sentences Ever Receive Clemency?

Many countries with the death penalty allow prisoners to seek *clemency*, in which case their sentence is commuted to a lesser penalty, such as life imprisonment. This may occur if there is some doubt about the defendant's guilt or because the government, for whatever reason, decides it wants to show mercy.

In Thailand, an appeal for clemency can be made to the king within 60 days of sentencing, after which he decides whether or not to offer a pardon. Between 1994 and 1998, 133

In March 2011, Illinois governor Pat Quinn signed a law that abolished the death penalty in his state. Quinn also commuted the sentences of 15 inmates remaining on Illinois's death row. They will now serve life in prison with no hope of parole. A longtime supporter of capital punishment, Quinn said that recent cases in which convictions were shown to be faulty had forced him to support the change. "If the system can't be guaranteed, 100-percent error-free, then we shouldn't have the system," he said. "It cannot stand."

Thai prisoners appealed to the king, and 50 were pardoned.

In 14 US states, the governor alone has the power to offer clemency, and in 11 states, the governor must decide only after hearing the recommendation of the Pardons Board or Advisory Group. In the case of federal prisoners, only the president can grant clemency. Since 1976, 223 death row inmates in the United States have been granted clemency. Reasons for this include doubts about guilt or the personal feelings of a particular governor about the death penalty process.

Death Row Conditions

Countries vary in the treatment of prisoners awaiting execution, but generally speaking, conditions are less comfortable than those for other prisoners. In Japan, death row inmates are

Personal Experiences

Willie Turner, who spent 17 years on death row in Virginia until his execution in May 1995, described his experience: "It is the unending, uninterrupted immersion in death that wears on you so much. It is the parade of friends and acquaintances who leave for the death house and never come back, while your own desperate and lonely time drains away. . . . It is watching yourself die over the years in the eyes of family and friends . . . I've spent over 5,000 days on death row. Not a single waking hour of any of those days has gone by without me thinking about my date with the executioner."

Robert Johnson described the toll of death row on prisoners in *Death Work* (2005): "The peculiar silence of death row stems from the empty and ultimately lifeless regime imposed on the condemned. These offenders, seen as unfit to live in even the prison community, are relegated to this prison within a prison . . . Worn down in small and almost imperceptible ways, they gradually become less than fully human. At the end, they give in, they give up, and submit: yielding themselves to the execution team and the machinery of death."

often kept in *manacles* for long periods, and visiting times for families and lawyers are severely restricted. In China, prisoners have both their hands and feet shackled, but death-row conditions are not a major public concern in this country, where death sentences are carried out relatively quickly.

In Zambia, prisoners with death sentences in the past faced severe overcrowding, with up to six men held in cells approxi-

An inmate in an overcrowded African prison must climb the bars of his cell to take a look outside.

mately 10 feet by 7 feet. According to Amnesty International, there have been several cases of tuberculosis but almost no access to medical treatment. Prisoners' uniforms were little more than rags. Similarly overcrowded and unhygienic conditions also exist in several Caribbean countries.

Death-row prisoners in the US do not have to face conditions as extreme as in other countries. However, condemned prisoners are held in a separate area from other prisoners and, in many cases, have fewer rights to exercise, education, and social time. One exception to this is Missouri, where prisoners under the death sentence form part of the prison's general population and have access to the same facilities.

Until the mid-1980s, most death-row prisoners in the US were confined to their cells for long periods and given very little opportunity for socializing or exercise. Various court cases have publicized these conditions, and states have instituted reforms to humanize death-row conditions. For example, in Texas, inmates regarded as capable of working are given jobs as well as the privileges of ordinary prisoners, though they are still separated from them. Those incapable of work (for mental, physical, or security reasons) are granted at least 15 hours per week of out-of-cell recreation time. This might include opportunities to exercise, dine with other death-row prisoners, or attend religious services.

Text-Dependent Questions

1. In what ways do death-row prisoners suffer due to long wait times until execution? How do families of the victims suffer because of the long wait times?

2. Why is it difficult for defense lawyers to make an appeal on a capital conviction case when given a limited time period?

 Research Project

Using the Internet or your school library, research the topic of death row prisoners, and answer the following question: "Should people on death row have the same rights as other prisoners?"

Some think that whatever their crimes, all prisoners are human beings and should be treated as such. There needs to be humane conditions for all people, including those on death row.

Others say that those who have committed murder did not have regard for someone else's life and have given up their own right to be treated fairly. They do not deserve the benefits of ordinary prison life that other inmates have.

Write a two-page report, using data you have found in your research to support your conclusion, and present it to your class.

The Future of
Capital Punishment

During the second half of the twentieth century, there was a worldwide trend towards the abolition of capital punishment. The question remains as to whether this trend will continue and result in the global abolition of the practice. Out of 196 countries, there are still 58 that retain the death penalty.

In a few countries, there has even been an extension of the death penalty to cover new crimes, such as currency *speculation* and terrorism. More than 30 countries have made drug *trafficking* a capital offense, and in Singapore, the death penalty is imposed for possessing even a small amount of illegal drugs. There are, however, signs that the application of the death penalty is in decline. Many of the countries that officially retain the death penalty actually employ this method of pun-

In the United States, prisoners often spend many years on death row. Since the 1980s, US courts have attempted to speed up executions by rejecting what they regard as excessive appeals, and laying down strict time limits by which appeals must be lodged.

In December 2007 the United Nations General Assembly adopted a resolution that called for a moratorium on executions to be established in all nations that still maintain the death penalty. The General Assembly has adopted similar resolutions reaffirming this stance in 2008, 2010, and 2012. Despite this, the United States and other nations continue to permit death sentences for certain crimes.

 Words to Understand in This Chapter

speculation—activity in which someone buys and sells things (such as stocks or pieces of property) in the hope of making a large profit but with the risk of a large loss.

trafficking—buying or selling something, especially illegally.

ishment quite rarely. In 2014, 22 countries out of 58 that retain the death penalty carried out executions. Not counting China, whose numbers are difficult to estimate because of state secrecy, three countries—Iran, Iraq, and Saudi Arabia—were responsible for 72 percent of the 607 recorded executions.

In the US, a large proportion—nearly three-quarters—of all executions since 1976 have occurred in just seven states. In other words, a change of policy in just a few countries and states would drastically reduce the number of people executed around the world.

Renzo Pomi of the non-governmental organization Amnesty International presents a report on the death penalty to members of the United Nations, April 2015.

Other countries and states have gone so far as to suspend the use of the death penalty in recent years, including Algeria, which announced a moratorium of the death penalty in 2012. This may well be the start of a trend—countries ending the use of capital punishment while still leaving themselves the option to reinstate it in future, should they decide to.

Capital punishment is a complicated issue because it involves many moral as well as practical questions. Do governments have the right to put people to death? Does the death penalty actually make society safer by removing certain criminals? Are there other forms of punishment that are fairer, both to the accused and the victim? There are no clear-cut answers to these questions, and the debate looks primed to continue for many years to come.

Text-Dependent Questions

1. Name four new crimes, besides murder, that can lead to capital punishment in some countries.
2. What three countries carry out four-fifths of executions in the world?
3. In countries like Algeria, what trend is beginning to take place regarding policy in capital punishment?

 Research Project

Using the Internet or your school library, research the topic of capital punishment and abolition, and answer the following question: "Should the public be able to decide on whether to retain or abolish the death penalty in their country?"

Some take the stance that in a democratic state, the people of that country should be allowed to decide on their own system of justice. They are the ones who most understand their culture, their people, and whether or not capital punishment is the best choice in their context.

Others maintain that capital punishment is an issue of universal human rights which should not be subject to the changeable moods of public opinion. There should be an international standard to abolish the death penalty that all countries should follow in order to prevent cruel and unusual punishment.

Write a two-page report, using data you have found in your research to support your conclusion, and present it to your class.

Appendix

Capital Punishment Legal Status by Country

The following countries retain the death penalty for ordinary crimes:

Afghanistan, Antigua and Barbuda, Bahamas, Bahrain, Bangladesh, Barbados, Belarus, Belize, Botswana, Chad, China, Comoros, Democratic Republic of the Congo, Cuba, Dominica, Egypt, Equatorial Guinea, Ethiopia, Gambia, Guatemala, Guinea, Guyana, India, Indonesia, Iran, Iraq, Jamaica, Japan, Jordan, Kuwait, Lebanon, Lesotho, Libya, Malaysia, Nigeria, North Korea, Oman, Pakistan, Palestine (State of), Qatar, Saint Kitts and Nevis, Saint Lucia, Saint Vincent and the Grenadines, Saudi Arabia, Singapore, Somalia, South Sudan, Sudan, Syria, Taiwan, Thailand, Trinidad and Tobago, Uganda, United Arab Emirates, United States of America, Vietnam, Yemen, Zimbabwe.

The following countries allow for the death penalty only in the case of "exceptional" crimes, such as crimes under military law or crimes committed in exceptional circumstances:

Armenia, Brazil, El Salvador, Fiji, Greece, Israel, Kyrgyzstan, Peru.

The following countries retain the death penalty for "ordinary" crimes (such as murder) but can be considered abolitionist in practice in that they have not executed anyone during the last 10 years and are believed to have a policy or established practice of not carrying out executions:

Algeria, Benin, Brunei Darussalam, Burkina Faso, Cameroon, Central African Republic, Republic of Congo, Eritrea, Grenada, Kenya, Laos, Liberia, Madagascar, Malawi, Maldives, Mali, Mauritania, Mongolia, Morocco, Myanmar, Nauru, Niger, Papua New Guinea, Russian Federation, Sierra Leone, South Korea, Sri Lanka, Suriname, Swaziland, Tajikistan, Tanzania, Tonga, Tunisia, Zambia.

In the following countries, the laws do not allow the death penalty to be imposed for any crime:

Albania, Andorra, Angola, Argentina, Australia, Austria, Azerbaijan, Belgium, Bosnia-Hezegovina, Bhutan, Bolivia, Bulgaria, Burundi, Cambodia, Canada, Cape Verde, Chile, Colombia, Costa Rica, Cote d'Ivoire, Croatia, Cyprus, Czech Republic, Denmark, Dominican Republic, East Timor, Ecuador, Estonia, Finland, France, Gabon, Georgia, Germany, Guinea-Bissau, Haiti, Honduras, Hungary, Iceland, Ireland, Italy, Latvia, Liechtenstein, Lithuania, Luxembourg, Macedonia, Malta, Mauritius, Mexico, Moldova, Monaco, Montenegro, Mozambique, Namibia, Nepal, Netherlands, New Zealand, Nicaragua, Norway, Paraguay, Philippines, Poland, Portugal, Romania, Rwanda, Samoa, San Marino, Senegal, Serbia, Slovak Republic, Slovenia, South Africa, Spain, Sweden, Switzerland, Togo, Turkey, Turkmenistan, Ukraine, UK, Uruguay, Uzbekistan, Vatican City State, Venezuela.

Recorded Executions of Child Offenders Since 1990

The following is a list of the names of all those under the age of 18 who have been executed since 1990. Following each name is the person's age, identified as either "ato" (at the time of the offense) or "ate" (at the time of execution). This data was provided by Amnesty International.

China
Zhao Lin, 16 ato (January 2003)
Gao Pan, 16 or 17 ato (March 8, 2004)

Dem Rep of Congo
Kasongo, 14 ate (January 15, 2000)

Iran
Kazem Shirafkan, 17 ate (1990)
Three juveniles, 16, 17, 17 ate (September 29,1992)
Manuchehr Taherian 16 ate (November 1995)
Ebrahim Qorbanzadeh, 17 ate (October 24, 1999)
Jassem Ebrahimi, 17 ate (October 14, 2000)
Mehrdad Yousefi, 16 ato (May 29, 2001)
Mohammad Mohammadzadeh, 17 ato (January 25, 2004)
Salman, 17 ato (May 12, 2004)
Atefeh Rajabi Sahaaleh, 16 ate (August 15, 2004)
Iman Farrokhi, 17 ato (January 19, 2005)

Ali Safarpour Rajabi, 16 or 17 ato (July 13, 2005)

Mahmoud Asghari, 15 or 16 ato (July 19, 2005)

Ayaz Marhoni, 16 or 17 ato (July 19, 2005)

Farshid Farighi, 14 to 16 ato (August 1, 2005)

Name unknown, 17 ate (August 23, 2005)

Name unknown, 17 ato (September 12, 2005)

Rostam Tajik, 16 ato (December 10, 2005)

Majid Segound (Sagvand), 17 ate (May 13, 2006)

Sattar, 17 ato (September 2006)

Morteza M, 16 ato (November 7, 2006)

Naser Batmani, under 18 ato (December 2006)

Mohammad Mousawi, 16 ato (April 22, 2007)

Sa'id Qanabar Zahi, 17 ato (May 27, 2007)

Mohammad Pezhman (Pejman), under 18 ato (May 29, 2007)

Amir Asgari, under 18 ato (October 10, 2007)

Hossein Gharabaghloo, 16 ato (October 17, 2007)

Babak Rahimi, 17 ato (October 17, 2007)

Two juveniles, under 18 ato (October 2007)

Mohamad Reza Tork, 16 ato (November 15, 2007)

Makwan Moloudzadeh, 13 ato (December 4, 2007)

Amir Hoshang Fazlollahzadeh, under 18 ato (December 31, 2007)

Javad Shojaee, 16 ato (February 26, 2008)

Mohammad Hassanzadeh, 16 or 17 ate (June 10, 2008)

Hasan Mozafar, under 18 ato (July 22, 2008)

Rahman Shahidi, under 18 ato (July 22, 2008)

Reza Hejazi, 15 ato (August 19, 2008)

Behnam Zare, 15 ato (August 26, 2008)

Gholamreza H, 17 ate (October 29, 2008)

Ahmad Zare, 17 ate (December 30, 2008)

Mola Gol Hassan, 17 ate (January 21, 2009)

Delara Darabi, 17 ate (May 1, 2009)

Ali Jafari, 17 ate (May 20, 2009)

Behnoud Shojaee, 17 ate (October 11, 2009)

Mosleh Zamani, 17 ate (December 17, 2009)

Mohammad A., 17 ate (July 10, 2010)

Two juveniles, A.N. and H.B., 17 ate (April 20, 2011)

Ali Reza Molla Soltani, 17 ato (September 21, 2011)

Nigeria

Chiebore Onuoha, 15 ato, 17 ate (July 31, 1997)

Pakistan

One juvenile, 17 ate (November 15, 1992)
Shamun Masih, 14 ato (September 30, 1997)
Ali Sher, 13 ato (November 3, 2001)
Mutabar Khan, 16 ato (June 13, 2006)

Saudi Arabia

Sadeq Mal-Allah, 17 when sentenced (September 3, 1992)
Dhahian Rakan al-Sibai'I, 15 or 16 ato (July 21, 2007)
Moeid bin Hussein Hakami, 16 ate (July 17, 2007)
Sultan Bin Sulayman Bin Muslim al-Muwallad, 17 ato (May 10, 2009)
'Issa bin Muhammad 'Umar Muhammad, 17 ato (May 10, 2009)
Rizana Nafeek, 17 ato (January 9, 2013)
Ali bin Muhammad bin Hazam al-Shihri, 16 ato (March 13, 2013)
Sa'id bin Nasser bin Muhammad al-Shahrani, 17 ato (March 2013)

Sudan

(Mohammed Jamal Gesmallah, 16 ato (August 31, 2005)
Imad Ali Abdullah, 17 ato (August 31, 2005)

United States

Dalton Prejean, 17 ato (May 18, 1990)
Johnny Garrett, 17 ato (February 11, 1992)
Curtis Harris, 17 ato (July 1, 1993)
Frederick Lashley, 17 ato (July 28, 1993)
Christopher Burger, 17 ato (December 7, 1993)
Ruben Cantu, 17 ato (August 24, 1993)
Joseph John. Cannon, 17 ato (April 22, 1998)
Robert Anthony Carter, 17 ato (May 18, 1998)
Sean Sellers, 16 ato (February 4, 1999)
Steve Roach, 17 ato (January 10, 2000)
Chris Thomas, 17 ato (January 13, 2000)
Glen McGinnis, 17 ato (January 25, 2000)

Gary Graham, 17 ato (June 22, 2000)

Gerald Mitchell, 17 ato (October 22, 2001)

Napolean Beazley, 17 ato (May 28, 2002)

TJ Jones, 17 ato (August 8, 2002)

Toronto Patterson, 17 ato (August 28, 2002)

Scott Allen Hain, 17 ato (April 3, 2003)

Yemen

Naseer Munir Nasser al'Kirbi, 13 ate (July 21, 1993)

Adil Muhammad, 16 ato (February 2007)

Saif alMa'amari, under 18 ato (January 21, 2012)

Fuad Ahmed Ali Abdulla, under 18 ato (January 2014)

Organizations Opposed to the Death Penalty

American Civil Liberties Union
125 Broad Street, 18th Floor
New York, NY 10004
Tel: (212) 549-2585
Website: https://www.aclu.org

Amnesty International
5 Penn Plaza, 16th Floor
New York, NY 10001
Tel: (212) 807-8400
Website: http://www.amnestyusa.org/

American Bar Association
Death Penalty Representation Project
321 North Clark Street
Chicago, IL 60654
Tel: (312) 988-5000
Website: www.americanbar.org/groups/committees/death_
penalty_representation.html

Citizens United for Alternatives to the Death Penalty
PMB 297,177 US Highway 1,
Tequesta, FL 33469
Tel: (800) 973-6548
Website: http://www.cuadp.org

Death Penalty Information Center
1015 18th Street NW, Suite 704
Washington, DC 20036
Tel: (202) 289-2275
Website: www.deathpenaltyinfo.org

Prison Activist Resource Center (PARC)
PO Box 70447
Oakland, CA 94612
Tel: (510) 893-4648
Website: https://www.prisonactivist.org/

Murder Victims Families for Reconciliation
PO Box 27764
Raleigh, NC 27611
Tel: (877) 896-4702
Website: www.mvfr.org

The National Coalition to Abolish the Death Penalty
1620 L Street, NW, Suite 250
Washington, DC 20036
Tel: (202) 331-4090
Website: http://www.ncadp.org

Organizations in Favor of the Death Penalty

Justice for All
9009 W 610 Loop
Houston, TX 77096
Tel: (713) 935-9300
Website: http://www.jfa.net/

National Center for Policy Analysis
14180 Dallas Parkway, Suite 350
Dallas, TX 75254
Tel: (972) 386-6272
Website: http://www.ncpa.org/

Series Glossary

apartheid—literally meaning "apartness," the political policies of the South African government from 1948 until the early 1990s designed to keep peoples segregated based on their color.

BCE and CE—alternatives to the traditional Western designation of calendar eras, which used the birth of Jesus as a dividing line. BCE stands for "Before the Common Era," and is equivalent to BC ("Before Christ"). Dates labeled CE, or "Common Era," are equivalent to *Anno Domini* (AD, or "the Year of Our Lord").

colony—a country or region ruled by another country.

democracy—a country in which the people can vote to choose those who govern them.

detention center—a place where people claiming asylum and refugee status are held while their case is investigated.

ethnic cleansing—an attempt to rid a country or region of a particular ethnic group. The term was first used to describe the attempt by Serb nationalists to rid Bosnia of Muslims.

house arrest—to be detained in your own home, rather than in prison, under the constant watch of police or other government forces, such as the army.

reformist—a person who wants to improve a country or an institution, such as the police force, by ridding it of abuses or faults.

republic—a country without a king or queen, such as the US.

United Nations—an international organization set up after the end of World War II to promote peace and co-operation throughout the world. Its predecessor was the League of Nations.

UN Security Council—the permanent committee of the United Nations that oversees its peacekeeping operations around the world.

World Bank—an international financial organization, connected to the United Nations. It is the largest source of financial aid to developing countries.

World War I—A war fought in Europe from 1914 to 1918, in which an alliance of nations that included Great Britain, France, Russia, Italy, and the United States defeated the alliance of Germany, Austria-Hungary, the Ottoman Empire, and Bulgaria.

World War II—A war fought in Europe, Africa, and Asia from 1939 to 1945, in which the Allied Powers (the United States, Great Britain, France, the Soviet Union, and China) worked together to defeat the Axis Powers (Germany, Italy, and Japan).

Further Reading

Bishop, Jeanne. *Change of Heart: Justice, Mercy, and Making Peace with My Sister's Killer*. Louisville: Westminster John Knox Press, 2015.

Bohm, Robert M. *Capital Punishment's Collateral Damage*. Durham: Carolina Academic Press, 2012.

Hood, Roger, and Carolyn Hoyle. *The Death Penalty: A Worldwide Perspective*. New York: Oxford University Press, 2015.

Madeira, Jody L. *Killing McVeigh: The Death Penalty and the Myth of Closure*. New York: New York University Press, 2012.

Moving Away from the Death Penalty: Arguments, Trends and Perspectives. New York: United Nations, 2014.

Stevenson, Bryan. *Just Mercy: A Story of Justice and Redemption*. New York: Spiegel & Grau, 2014.

Internet Resources

https://www.amnesty.org/en/what-we-do/death-penalty/
Amnesty International campaigns against the death penalty. Its website is packed with facts and figures, historical and current, about the death penalty worldwide.

www.deathpenaltyinfo.org
The Death Penalty Information Center is against capital punishment. Its website provides articles, facts, reports, and demographic statistics about the death penalty, mainly in the US.

http://deathpenalty.procon.org/
This website provides side-by-side arguments for and against capital punishment on its ethical, legal, and social issues.

http://www.deathpenaltyworldwide.org/index.cfm
Death Penalty Worldwide is a database developed by Cornell Law School that has capital punishment statistics (countries' legal stances, number of executions per year, methods of execution, crimes punishable by death) for countries worldwide.

http://www.religioustolerance.org/execute.htm

This website has information on capital punishment and arguments for and against, including religious perspectives on the issue.

http://www.mvfr.org/

The Murder Victims' Families for Reconciliation actively campaigns against the death penalty with the belief that executions do not facilitate healing. The website has personal stories, videos, and resources for victims' families.

Index

Numbers in ***bold italics*** refer to captions.

About the Author

Adam Ward studied history at Liberty College and worked with Amnesty International. This is his first book for young people.

Picture Credits: California Department of Corrections and Rehabilitation: 9; Everett Collection: 22, 24, 33, 53; State of Texas/DeathPenaltyInfo.org: 6; Florida Department of Corrections: 76, 79; used under license from Shutterstock, Inc.: 2, 12, 17, 18, 19, 21, 28, 39, 43, 47, 50, 65, 66, 72, 105; Philip Chidell / Shutterstock.com: 32; Robert J. Daveant / Shutterstock.com: 1, 31, 62, 86; Mohamed Elsayyed / Shutterstock.com: 58; Botond Horvath / Shutterstock.com: 60; Anton_Ivanov / Shutterstock.com: 69; A. Katz / Shutterstock.com: 35; Nagel Photography / Shutterstock.com: 14, 25, 100; Renata Sedmakova / Shutterstock.com: 16; Rena Schild / Shutterstock.com: 40; United Nations photo: 44, 54, 83, 88, 89; US Department of Defense: 34, 57; White House photo: 81; Wikimedia Commons: 37.